Manage your time

How to work more effectively

A & C Black • London

D0299199

Revised edition first published in Great Britain in 2010

A & C Black Publishers Ltd
36 Soho Square
London W1D 3QY
www.acblack.com

Copyright © A & C Black Publishers Ltd, 2010

First edition 2004 © Bloomsbury Publishing, 2004
Reprinted 2007 by A & C Black Publishers Ltd

A CIP record for this book is available from the British Library.

ISBN: 9–781–4081–2800–8

This book is produced using paper that is made from wood grown in managed, sustainable forests. It is natural, renewable and recyclable. The logging and manufacturing processes conform to the environmental regulations of the country of origin.

Design by Fiona Pike, Pike Design, Winchester
Typeset by RefineCatch Limited, Bungay, Suffolk
Printed in Spain by GraphyCems

Contents

How well do you manage your time?

Answer the questions and work out your time management profile, then read the guidance points for ideas on how to make more effective use of your time.

How often do your tasks take longer than expected?

a) Hardly ever   b) Sometimes   c) Regularly

How often do you clear out your desk and e-mails?

a) Regularly   b) Seldom   c) Hardly ever

How would you rate your delegating skills?

a) Good   b) Average   c) Poor

When you plan a meeting do you schedule in extra time in case it overruns?

a) Always   b) Sometimes   c) Never

How often do you work late?

a) Hardly ever   b) Sometimes   c) Almost always

How often do you make commitments that you can't stick to?

a) Hardly ever   b) Sometimes   c) Regularly

How often do you say 'no' when asked to do things you have no time for?

a) Regularly   b) Sometimes   c) Hardly ever

When given a task, do you ask for a deadline?

a) Always   b) Sometimes   c) Never

How often do you schedule in time for yourself?

a) Every day   b) Every week   c) Never

How do you react when someone chases you for a project that you have put on the back burner?

a) Explain why I had to prioritise other jobs
b) Feel guilty that it has been delayed and do it ASAP
c) Panic – I had almost forgotten about it

How do you plan your daily tasks?

a) I write out a daily schedule and stick to it
b) I make a list of the most important tasks and hope to remember the others
c) I tackle jobs as they come up

What do you do when faced with many projects?

a) Get on with the most important ones first
b) Choose the most interesting job and start on that
c) Start several tasks and continue with the easiest one

How organised is your work space?

a) Very. I know where everything is.
b) Fairly. I have been known to lose things.
c) Not at all. I don't think about the state of my desk!

a = 1, b = 2 and c = 3. Now add up your scores.

Chapter **1** is useful to everyone as it will help build awareness of the ways in which you spend your time, and of pockets of 'lost' time that you can regain.

■ **13–20:** You manage your time well already, but remember to leave space for self-development, and time to switch off – it's possible you have become over-efficient or inflexible! Chapter **6** gives you hints on managing your work–life balance. It is also important not to be too controlling – remember to delegate so others can develop their skills too as well as relieve the burden on you (Chapter **3**).

■ **21–31:** You have a reasonably balanced approach to your working life, but make sure your good intentions regarding time management come to fruition. Conduct a 'time audit' (Chapter **1**) and avoid spending long hours at work as this will end up making you tired and less efficient. To make the best use of your day, manage the time you spend in meetings (Chapter **4**) and learn how to keep on top of the many e-mails that come your way (Chapter **5**).

■ **32–39:** You're at risk of becoming exhausted and doing a bad job because your time is being used so inefficiently. You need to make major changes in the way you work. Don't underestimate how long tasks will take – wishful thinking means nothing when you're about to miss a deadline! Learn to manage both e-mails and information by reading Chapters **2** and **5**. Chapter **7** will help you develop decision-making skills so you don't waste time procrastinating.

Organising your time

Time management is about making every moment effective by being truly focused and not dividing your energies by worrying about the past or future. However, it's still important to be able to keep the past, present and future in perspective so that you can plan and prioritise effectively. In this way you're able to set tasks in the right context. This gives a sense of order, structure and security for those who are dependent upon your time management skills.

In our working lives, time is the one thing that is in ever increasing demand. Many tools are now available that offer instant access to information and each other, the idea being that more time is released for increased efficiency and productivity. Although these tools are designed to save time, they can be so complex that they use up a great deal of time and as a result put additional pressures on managers.

Step one: Conduct a 'time audit'

✔ As a first step towards organising your time well, do a 'time audit' on your life. What is the balance between the demands that are placed upon you at work and the obligations and pleasures that define your private life? Does this balance satisfy you, or do you find yourself sacrificing one activity or part of your life for another?

The key to good time management is being aware of the world in which you live and the interrelationships between the component parts, then choosing how you divide your time between each one.

How to do a time audit

1 Take a large sheet of paper and write your name at the centre.

2 Place words around your name that represent the demands upon your life. Include contracted work hours, travelling/commuting time, social hours at work – lunches, dinners, and post-work socialising – and family commitments, remembering that your time demands are likely to increase according to the number of children/dependents that you have. Also include your wider family and friends, sporting or fitness activities, socialising time and time spent on hobbies or areas of personal interest.

3 Mark on the sheet the number of hours that are dedicated to each of these areas throughout the day. (You may want to use half-hour intervals if you think they'd be more meaningful.) For example, you may

have: work (8), commuting (2), picking up children from school (0.5) and so on. This will graphically represent your life in terms of the choices and trade-offs you're making in those areas that are important to you.

4 Ask yourself, 'Is this how I want to live my life?' You may sacrifice some important areas of your life in the short term, but be aware of what happens when a particular phase of your life comes to an end. How will you manage this transition, particularly when it's unexpected or sudden, such as a change in work circumstances or retirement?

5 Take a highlighter pen and mark those areas on your chart that need attention. If, for instance, you feel you're spending too much time at work, you need to re-establish the objectives of your role and the demands placed upon you by others. Perhaps it's time for you to think about requesting flexible working hours, for example. Evaluate how you're going to get a better balance. Some of the time management toolkits outlined on page 8 will give you ideas on how to do this.

Step two: Make adjustments

1 Be aware of your choices

The desire to improve your time management skills is half the battle but you need to be aware of the choices you have to make. These relate to your overall life balance and the values you hold.

✔ Look at what you're being asked to do at work and why. Is this because it's related to your role or because you hold a particular skill or expertise? If you're being asked to do many things outside your area of responsibility, you may need to speak to your boss to clarify your job boundaries.

There are always choices to be made. You may find that you can win more time by avoiding time spent on commuting and working from home. However, make sure that your family doesn't automatically see this as additional time you'll be able to spend with them. You will need to create boundaries to ensure that your productivity remains high and that this new environment does not disrupt your efforts.

TOP TIP
Don't make commitments that you know you can't meet. If you're concerned about a potential time conflict, talk to the people involved rather than waste more time by worrying about it.

---

2 Plan for lost time

✔ Look at your chart and see the effects of unpredictable delays and how they can affect the rest of your day or week.

Lost time accumulated over a period has a surprisingly large impact on the time available for other activities. You get a 'build-up' of negative time. If you can, plan pockets of space in your day to accommodate them. This releases pressure and allows you to get back on track.

TOP TIP

If you use any time management systems, start off simply for a better chance of success. You may find you have to manage expectations better. Build in some slack when you plan schedules so that you don't back yourself into a corner. Sometimes when people are aware of your timings, they build in slack as well.

---

3 Be prepared to change behavioural habits

✓ Be aware of any patterns that characterise the way you manage your time. You may find that you're constantly overrunning in meetings (see Chapter 4, 'Managing meetings') or that you pick up a lot of spurious work because you aren't assertive enough in saying 'no'. Both these consume time that you may not have available.

Dealing with disorganised team members

In order to run an efficient team, every person in the team needs to know exactly what they're doing and how that fits into what everybody else is doing.

✔ If a team member is disorganised, you need to get this person to stand back from what they're doing and look at the patterns or behaviour they're exhibiting and the deadlines they and the department are working to. How does this person's contribution fit in and what are his or her priorities?

Often time management requires a change in habitual behaviour. For this reason, you cannot expect to become a good time manager overnight. Learning the skills is one thing, using them is another – it takes time and can only be achieved by building awareness, charting a clear route and rewarding success.

TOP TIP

Be as honest as you can about how long things take. Overestimating the amount of time needed can be counterproductive: you might end up panicking because it looks as if you can't possibly fit everything in. But underestimating can be just as dangerous – you run the risk of feeling that you're forever catching up. So get into the habit of jotting down how long it takes you to do regular tasks. Then when you need to plan your day in detail, you'll be better equipped to make an accurate estimate of how long things take.

Step three: Prioritise and plan ahead

✔ Look at your workload and categorise your tasks into those that are important to your overall role, those which will add benefit to your role but may not be central and those things that you do that you may be good at but which are outside your area of responsibility.

✔ Set yourself definite and specific goals. What do you want to achieve in the time that you have? It is best to write these goals down. Make sure that they are achievable and set yourself a realistic time limit in which to achieve them. It may help to divide the task up so that you can take it step by step. This will make the completion of the task more rewarding, as you can measure your progress on the way.

We often get caught up in responding to others' expectations and sacrificing our own choices. As you undertake your time audit, make sure that you're not spending time on unnecessary activities that don't serve your purpose. Delegate wherever you can but don't expect others to do what you can't do or pick up the mess you leave behind you.

The central point is that planning is essential. It will help you prioritise, anticipate problems and potential conflicts and see where you're going. Be aware of time pressures as you plan. Awareness must always precede action.

Time management toolkits

There are a number of time management toolkits that help people order their days but they're only as useful as the time invested in using them. Many time management courses teach you how to use processes to prioritise your tasks and activities. Remember that your view of what is a priority may be different from someone else's. In using these toolkits, remember to spend some time talking to all the relevant people involved at work to make sure that misunderstandings don't occur.

Some commercially available toolkits and techniques include:

- BlackBerrys® or iPhones
- organisers
- 'to do' lists
- categorising work according to its level of importance and focusing only on the essential
- aligning tasks to business goals and objectives and cutting out the 'nice to do'
- shared diaries – team, secretarial, professional groups

It's not easy to make the transition from depending on a diary and Post-It™ notes to organising your life with a computerised device such as a BlackBerry® or iPhone.

✔ Plan the time it will take to learn the new technology and transfer your information. Only allow a month during which you use a dual system then throw the paper diary away.

New technology can be intimidating, but where there's a will, there's a way. You will soon find your new system as convenient as any other you may have used in the past, if not more so.

TOP TIP

Always plan ahead and try to anticipate the pressure of commitments that you make. Make sure that as you plan, you not only build in time for reflecting and learning, but you build in time for yourself.

Common mistakes

✗ You buy a new gadget that you don't need or want

In moments of desperation, people often rush out and buy the latest time management technology, which can be both expensive and complicated to use. It is always worth considering what is motivating you to make that purchase. You cannot impose a system when deep down, you're not completely convinced it will help. It is much better to take time to get to the root of the problem and see what the cause is. Once this has been established, the most suitable approach to time management may be identified.

✗ You expect too much of yourself and become disenchanted

A new environment takes some getting used to. When we try to change too many things at once, pressure is bound to cause us to step back into old habits. While the logic in time management appears straightforward, the complexity of our lives means that managing time is not straightforward. The answer is to take small steps, heading towards clear goals.

✗ You're not prepared to break bad habits and don't ask for help from family and colleagues

We all know people who are always late or people who are always early. The way you plan your life and time rapidly takes on a pattern. Breaking that pattern can mean that we have to change the way we view ourselves, view the world in which we live and ask for help and support from others in making that change.

STEPS TO SUCCESS

✔ Time management is about making the *most effective* use of your time, both at home and at work.

✔ Awareness is all. Being aware of how you apportion your time, and how those around you spend theirs, is essential for good time management.

✔ A good place to start is to conduct a 'time audit', which will help to make you more aware of the balance between your work life and personal life, and between the different jobs you do at work.

✔ Remember that there are always choices to be made – and be prepared to make them. Change the habits of a lifetime!

✔ Define your goals – this is an essential part of the prioritising and planning process. Make sure they are specific, realistic and measurable.

✔ You cannot plan your time down to the last minute. Be honest about the amount of time tasks are likely to take, and set aside time to allow for unexpected delays.

✔ Don't try to make all the changes at once – you will be far more likely to slip back into your old habits. Build them up over time and you will soon see the difference.

Useful links

ISYS Intelligent Systems:
www.isys-group.co.uk
Mindtools.com:
www.mindtools.com/pages/main/newMN_HTE.htm
Time Management Guide:
www.time-management-guide.com
Total Success, Time Management training programmes:
www.tsuccess.dircon.co.uk/timemanagementtips.htm

Avoiding information overload

The amount of information available to us is rapidly increasing. Accordingly, we are all expected to absorb and respond to more information than ever before. There are a number of reasons for this.

- The speed with which customers expect to complete transactions has increased. They work on a just-in-time basis, no longer waiting for paperwork to pass through several sets of hands before taking action.
- Technology now allows for the instantaneous transfer of information to everyone's PC.
- Fewer people are employed to manage information. Many secretaries and personal assistants have been replaced by laptops and PDAs.
- Globalisation and deregulation have given rise to new opportunities, but they have also increased competition and the need to understand the changing market.
- Business structures have changed so that many projects are now outsourced, demanding clear and rapid communication.
- There are many means of instant communication and data access. The BlackBerry®, Internet, e-mail and tele- or

videoconferencing have all contributed to the
vast and fast flow of information.

The problem is that we have all had to deal with
this influx without any preparation, training or
time! Often, we find it difficult to process the
flood of information – we feel as though we're
drowning, struggling to find time for more
important tasks. The good news is that there
are steps you can take to keep your head above
water.

The scale of the problem

Although information overload is a fairly recent
phenomenon, it has already claimed casualties.
Managers often feel that they have to keep up with the
information flow in order to perform well, yet increasing
amounts of time are required to enable them to get
through the massive amounts of data available. This time
pressure is resulting in stress and, in some cases,
burnout. A worldwide survey conducted by Reuters
found that two thirds of managers suffer from increased
tension and one third from ill health because of
information overload. Stress causes:

- increased levels of anxiety;
- a reduction in decision-making capabilities;
- problems with short-term memory;
- a reduced ability to concentrate.

This isn't a good recipe for management excellence. There are, however, ways you can reduce the burden.

Step one: Take control of the problem

Information management, like time management, is a matter of discipline. You need to set boundaries around how much time you're prepared to spend processing information.

✔ Decide what your limits are and create a personal information management system that works for you. This may be setting boundaries around the time you spend responding to e-mails, filtering them through your assistant (if you're lucky enough to have one), or responding only to those e-mails that hold high importance for you.

TOP TIP

Draw up some criteria that determine what you allow through your filter and what you exclude. This may mean putting priorities on your e-mails and deleting those that are low priority, returning calls only to those people you need to speak to, and only looking at a piece of data once before deciding what to do with it. If you miss something important, you can be sure that it will come back to you.

✔ Identify any time-wasting information and eliminate it. Ask to be removed from the list of often unnecessary 'All staff' e-mails; request a good spam filter from the IT department; ask for a summary of overly long minutes or reports.

Step two: Seek information efficiently

✔ Aim for the 'Pareto principle' when seeking information. In other words, 20 per cent of what has been accessed probably holds 80 per cent of the information you need. It's anxiety that propels people to spend excessive time wading through every piece of data available. People used to make decisions in ambiguous situations; it was considered to be a management skill. Aim for developing your instincts along with your knowledge.

✔ Find your own preferred places for accessing information and discipline yourself to go there only. You already know which are the quality sites for your particular field of work. Failing this, you could make use of the information officers in the library of your professional body. They are experienced at finding relevant information and can often save you a great deal of time.

✔ Only look at data that is relevant to your job, the project you're working on or the decision you're making. Resist the temptation to be intrigued by those things that lie outside your area of responsibility. Too often, people are sucked into irrelevant detail because they don't know where to draw the line.

TOP TIP

The advantage and disadvantage of the Web is that it's freely available – anyone can set up a website, whether it's poor quality or not, and you can spend hours getting lost in useless websites while looking for the high-quality information you need. Being more specific in your searches will reduce the time that you waste looking for the information you want, as will adding the most productive sites to your list of Favourites. Otherwise, you may want to set time boundaries around your Web searches, knowing that you will probably pick up most of the information you need in the first ten minutes or so.

Step three: Learn to say 'no'

✔ Try not to be the dumping ground for information that others don't want to wade through. Many will try to pass the burden on to you if you even hint at being receptive to the task. Take control of what passes over your desk and decide not to be held to ransom by a piece of data.

✔ Limit your availability. Leave your mobile phone switched off for periods during the day when you can be quiet and restful or let your voicemail field calls for you. This way you can determine who to speak to and when to schedule the conversations. Anyone who needs to speak to you urgently will find a way of getting through to you.

Step four: Regulate information

✔ Learn to throw things away. Have the courage to throw data away or delete files when you have exhausted their usefulness. You can always access the same data again and, probably when you do, it will have been updated.

✔ Use the principles of time management as these will help with information overload. Surfing the Web is incredibly seductive, with each link taking you further and further into fascinating but unnecessary detail. Decide how much time you'll spend in each session, print the information that is relevant and leave the rest in the ether. You often pick up all the information you need in a few hits, the remainder being less fruitful.

TOP TIP

It may seem rather self-defeating to resort to technology to solve a problem that technology produced in the first place, but there are

**useful electronic devices that can help
alleviate information overload such as the
BlackBerry® or iPhone. Their functions
can be accessed while travelling, making
use of otherwise 'dead' time: you can read
your e-mails, edit documents, plan meetings,
write reports and even read the newspaper.
Any changes can be automatically transferred
to your PC when you get back to the office.**

Common mistakes

✗ You get bogged down in detail

Getting drawn into the detail of all the information that's available wastes a lot of time. People often fear they'll miss an essential piece of information if they don't comb through every possible source. In fact this rarely happens. Resist the temptation to scutinise every single piece of information that appears on your screen or arrives on your desk.

✗ You fail to prioritise

Being able to prioritise information will save you hours. Some pieces will need detailed analysis, others just a quick skim. You may even find that you can delegate some of the processing to a member of your team, outlining what they should focus on and when they should report back to you. Remember to give clear instructions and to set an attainable deadline.

✗ You never switch off

Not being able to switch off from the need to absorb or generate information can be tiring and stressful. Blood pressure can rise, mental faculties can deteriorate and any patience you may have had can disappear altogether. Just as the body needs time to relax, so does the mind – and not just when you're asleep. Quieting the mind through techniques such as meditation or yoga has been proven to increase health, improve memory and stimulate creativity. It's also been linked to increased productivity and a sense of wellbeing. If this doesn't appeal, try other recuperative pursuits such as listening to music, reading or taking gentle exercise. Anything that allows the mind to 'freewheel' will prove beneficial.

STEPS TO SUCCESS

✔ People often feel that in order to perform well they have to spend more and more time going through the huge amount of information being passed around electronically. It's just not true.

✔ Developing a personal information management system will help you keep afloat amid the flood of information.

✔ It's important to be selective in the sources you use. Don't be drawn into the tangle of irrelevant information on the Internet – choose your favourites carefully, then use them!

✔ Employ technology to control the flow of information – divert e-mails, use voicemail and switch your mobile phone off to prevent interruptions.

✔ Remember to throw printouts away and delete files and e-mails when you have finished with them. There is no need to hoard information – if it's important it can always be found again.

✔ In order to absorb data effectively you must learn to 'switch off' and give your mind the chance to digest the information.

Useful links

InfoWorld business resources:
www.infoworld.com
iPhone:
www.apple.com/uk/iphone
BlackBerry:
http://uk.blackberry.com

Delegating tasks

Mastering the skill of delegation will help you manage your time and therefore give you more freedom to concentrate on your priorities. But it's often when we are most pushed for time that we delegate least. It's easy to panic and to cut yourself off from your colleagues or employees when you need their support the most.

However, delegation isn't just about making your workload lighter by giving tasks to others. It's also about getting staff to take full responsibility for certain key duties. In order for a business to grow and for employees to find new paths of development, new people must be employed to take over established functions, releasing others to develop different aspects of the business.

Benefits of delegation

- **Time management.** You'll have more time to deal with the problems and tasks at the top of your priority list, allowing you to feel more in control.
- **Personal effectiveness.** Delegating tasks allows you to concentrate on the things you do best, and will give you the chance to tackle more interesting and challenging tasks in the future.

- **Growth.** Passing tasks down the line is essential if the business is to grow. Not knowing how to do this is recognised as one of the biggest obstacles to business growth, particularly in small businesses. You should have more time available to think strategically about business growth.

- **Staff development.** If staff are to develop, they need new challenges. Delegation helps you test out their ability to increase their contribution to the business. Staff can take quick decisions themselves, and will often have a better understanding of the details concerned. Good delegation should improve the overall productivity of employees and boost their morale.

- **Management.** Dealing with staff may seem a difficult problem, but that is what management is all about. It is too easy to withdraw into 'essential' tasks and not develop relations with staff. The bottom line is that it's wasteful for senior staff to spend their time doing low value work.

Delegation isn't always the easiest option. But while it doesn't necessarily make everything easier (there will always be other challenges), it does tend to make things more efficient and effective. It is essentially a more interactive way of working with a team of people, involving instruction, training and development. You'll need to invest some time and effort to do it effectively, but the long-term benefits will make it worth your while.

Step one: Know when to delegate

Delegation is fundamental to management, so look for opportunities to do it. These may include:

- when you have too much work to do to complete all your tasks;
- when you don't have enough time to devote to all-important tasks;
- when it's clear that certain staff need to develop, particularly new employees;
- when an employee has the skills needed to perform a specific task.

Step two: Know what to delegate

✔ Delegate the routine administrative tasks that take up too much of your time. There may be small everyday things which you've always done, which you may even enjoy doing, but which are an inappropriate use of time.

✔ Delegate projects which it makes sense for one person to handle. These will be a good test of how a person manages and co-ordinates their work. Give the person something they can do, rather than impossible tasks at which others have failed. That might be a damaging experience for the person concerned.

✔ Delegate tasks for which an employee has a special aptitude. Make the most of your team's skills.

✔ Don't get bogged down in relationship management. Liaising with a particular person or organisation is an important but often time-consuming task. It can be delegated.

Step three: Know whom to delegate to

Staff development is a vital part of delegation. It is therefore very important to have a good understanding of the people you can delegate tasks to. The approach should be adapted according to the individual. They must have the skills and ability or at least the potential to develop into the role, and they must also be someone that can be trusted.

✔ Test employees with small tasks to help show you what they can do. Do they show good time management skills themselves? Do they keep a diary? Do they make notes? Training may be given or these skills developed in the person through delegation.

✔ The employee must be available for the assignment, and the people who do effective work should not be overburdened.

✔ Try to delegate tasks out among as many employees as possible, and remember to consider the option of assigning a task to two or more people.

TOP TIP
Don't delegate a task and its attendant
responsibilities without also giving
the relevant people the necessary
authority to complete the task.
Don't hinder their progress!

Step four: Delegate interactively

✔ Think positively. As a manager you have the right
and an obligation to delegate. It won't happen
perfectly first time. Your ability to delegate will
improve with experience. Try to act decisively and
avoid prevarication – you may need to learn more
assertiveness skills. A positive approach will also
give the person you're delegating to confidence in
themselves. It's important for them to feel that you
believe in them.

TOP TIP
Be patient and have faith in the people around
you. One of the reasons you're delegating is
to relieve yourself of stress, not to add to
your burden by constantly worrying about
whether the person is doing a good job.

✔ Plan ahead. If you expect the person to be efficient, you'll
need to make sure that you yourself are well organised. If

there is no overall plan of what is going on, it will be hard to identify, schedule and evaluate the work you've asked others to do. Schedule time to develop and assess the person in the job. Do you have a plan for their development? Are there notes about how they're doing? You'll need to assess the task and then decide how much responsibility the person should be given. Prepare before seeing the person, but don't use this as a pretext for delay.

✔ Discuss the tasks and problems in depth with the person you're delegating to, and explain clearly what is expected of them. It's crucial to give precise objectives, but a manager may choose to encourage the person to seek these out themselves by letting them ask questions. Employees should participate in setting the parameters. They need to understand why they're doing the task, where it fits into the scheme of things. Ask them how they will go about the task, discuss the plan and the support they might need.

✔ Set deadlines and schedule them into diaries. Summarise what has been agreed and take notes about what each employee is required to do. If the person is given a lot of creative scope and is being tested out, you may decide to be deliberately vague. If the task is urgent and critical, it will be essential to be specific. If you're nervous about their ability to handle the work, make sure they know you are available for support (see **Step five**).

Step five: Follow up with support and reward

✔ Back up your employees. The degree of support you give will depend upon the development of the person, and your relationship with them. In the early stages it can be appropriate to work with the person, to share certain tasks. You'll be able to back off more as your understanding of their abilities increases. Encourage them to come back if they have difficulties. While it's important to have time to yourself, you need to be accessible if the person has a problem. But try not to interfere or criticise if things are going according to plan.

TOP TIP

Focus on results rather than methods. If the person you're delegating to doesn't carry out the task in the way you would have done, don't rush to take over or start butting in. Your way works best for you, but it may not work so well for someone else.

✔ Monitor progress. It is too easy to forget about the task until the deadline looms. In the meantime, all sorts of things could have gone wrong. When planning, build in time to review progress. If more problems were expected to arise and nothing has been heard then you may want to check with the employee.

Schedule in routine meetings. Deadlines and objectives may have to be altered as the situation changes.

✔ Review performance. You can discuss career development issues in appraisals, and note the results of delegated tasks for this purpose. When a task is complete remember to give praise and review how it went. If the person has failed to deliver, this should also be discussed.

✔ Reward achievement. If a person's responsibilities are increased, they should receive fair rewards for it. On the other hand, there may be limits on what you can offer, so don't get carried away and promise rewards if they can't be delivered. Rewards might depend upon the overall success of the business

Common mistakes

✘ **You doubt your employees' ability**
You fear that the delegatee will create even more problems than they solve. You must learn to trust your team. Even if they make a mistake they will benefit from the experience in the long run, and therefore so will you.

✘ **You think delegation wastes time**
It seems quicker to do the task yourself than to bother explaining it and correcting mistakes. This may be true, but as you progress up the career ladder, you'll need to delegate more, so the earlier you start, the better.

✗ **You worry about your status**

An employee who is quick on the uptake and does well can take over the role of being the person everyone goes to with their problems. Maybe you feel threatened by their competence. They may even find something wrong with the way you do things. Remember that you do a good job too and have found someone you can rely on when time is tight.

✗ **You lack confidence**

If problems arise, or if the person fails to discharge their responsibilities, you may doubt your own ability to confront the person about their actions. Break out of this vicious circle by making an active attempt to improve your communication skills.

✗ **You neglect staff development**

Remember that delegation not only benefits you by freeing up some of your time, but will give your staff a sense of achievement by earning your trust and developing new skills. This will improve the effectiveness of the whole team, and so the success of the organisation.

STEPS TO SUCCESS

✔ Mastering the skill of delegation will mean that everyone benefits – it will help you manage your time and it will aid staff development, improving overall productivity.

✔ Don't let tight schedules get in the way of delegation. When you're under pressure, passing tasks on – to the right person – will save you time in the end.

✔ Remember to delegate interactively – get to know your staff, listen to their worries and discover their strengths.

✔ Successfully passing responsibility down the line is essential for company growth.

✔ Remember to delegate assertively. Your confidence will be transferred on to the person you're delegating to.

✔ Don't forget that when you delegate, you remain ultimately responsible for the results of the work you have delegated.

Useful links

businessballs.com:
www.businessballs.com/delegation.htm
Mindtools.com:
www.mindtools.com/tmdelegt.html
Getahead-direct.com:
www.getahead-direct.com/gwtm07-successful-delegation.htm

4

Managing meetings

Meetings are a necessary evil in everyone's working life. Handled well, they can help those gathered get to the bottom of a tricky situation, agree actions and do something positive. Handled badly, they can be a terrific waste of time. Basically, you want to get in and out as soon as possible with the relevant decisions made so that you can get on with the rest of your day.

This chapter offers advice for anyone who has to plan and chair a meeting. Special arrangements need to be followed for large meetings such as board meetings or annual general meetings, so in this chapter we focus only on the type of meeting held most commonly in an everyday work situation.

Step one: Decide if you really need a meeting

In some cases, meetings are not always a good use of people's time and effort.

✔ If someone suggests that a meeting be held to discuss an issue related to your project, team or department, think hard about whether gathering the attendees in one place is really the most efficient way forward.

There may be more time-saving alternatives to gathering everyone together for a meeting. For example, you could try:

■ conference calls or videoconferencing. If you have access to these facilities, or can afford them, they offer a good way of holding a discussion without having to disrupt the attendees' day too much.

■ discussing the issue via e-mail by sending a message to all relevant parties. Your e-mail should set out the issue clearly, ask for a response and give a deadline – and double-check that you have included everyone before sending it!

If all else fails, and a face-to-face meeting seems to be the best and least unwieldy way of agreeing action on the issue at hand, prepare as much as you can in advance and delegate where appropriate.

TOP TIP
Think carefully about the type of meeting you need. Brainstorming sessions or creative discussions often don't fit conveniently into well-planned timetables so may be best slotted into a less hectic part of the year.

Step two: Do the initial planning

1 Think carefully about who to invite

To avoid wasting the company time and money, you should try to limit the numbers by only inviting those who really need to be there. These will be people directly involved in the decisions that need to be taken during the meeting, those significantly affected by those actions or those who have some specific knowledge to contribute.

✔ The most productive meetings are usually those with the fewest number of people attending. Make sure you keep the numbers down.

✔ If the agenda is lengthy and covers a variety of issues, there are two options: you could consider asking people to drop in and out when their relevant section comes up; or you might want to consider a series of smaller meetings.

2 Give the attendees all the relevant information in good time

To make sure that all the attendees have a chance to raise their concerns during the meeting, give them plenty of notice of the meeting's time and venue and circulate a draft agenda outlining the topics to be discussed and the time limits assigned to each topic.

TOP TIP

It is vital that all the attendees are clear about the purpose of the meeting and why they have been called together. The agenda should set out what needs to be accomplished between the start and finish of the meeting.

Time limits create a healthy sense of urgency. By stipulating the start and finish time of the meeting, as well as setting time limits for each topic on the agenda (particularly important if you are holding a lengthy meeting and asking people to drop in and out), you will encourage people to stay focused. Sticking to these time fixtures is essential, of course, for this to work!

Other information you should provide your attendees with prior to the meeting includes:

- Directions to the venue in case they haven't been there before.
- Information on who else is attending (this will be particularly helpful if you are going to be joined by people external to your company such as consultants or freelance contributors).
- Background information or documents relevant to the meeting. For example, if you are going to discuss a long-overdue overhaul of your product catalogue, send everyone a copy of your existing catalogue in case they no longer have copies of the original. You could also

include other similar publications whose style you admire
to see if anyone can think of new ways of presenting your
products.

■ Your contact details and those of one other person in the
office (such as your assistant, if you have one) in case
of emergency.

3 Think about catering requirements

✔ If you think your meeting will take longer than a few
hours or is likely to take place over lunch, remember to
ask all attendees whether they have any special dietary
requirements. This will save a lot of time and stress on
the day.

TOP TIP
**Research shows that the best time to hold a
meeting is just before lunch or towards the
end of the day. This motivates attendees to
focus on the agenda and keep time!**

---

4 Delegate taking the minutes

Try to find someone other than yourself to take the
minutes. This will free you up to steer the meeting as
appropriate.

✔ If the person designated as the minute-taker is new to
the project or issue you're going to discuss, run through
some key words or acronyms associated with the task at

hand so that he or she is not baffled by the jargon –
you and the other attendees may be well versed in the
relevant vocabulary, but don't expect the same from
a 'newcomer'.

Step three: Find and prepare the venue

✔ Once you know that a formal meeting is on the cards,
find an appropriate space in which the meeting can be
held. Some companies have a 'booking system' for
meeting rooms, so give yourself enough time when
planning the meeting date to make sure that you can
get an appropriately sized room for when you want.
Don't assume it'll just be free as and when you're
ready!

✔ Give yourself (or your assistant if you have one) plenty of
time to get the room ready as the meeting gets closer. In
particular make sure that:

- the room is tidy;
- you've enough tables and chairs to accommodate
  everyone;
- if you're using one, the flip chart has enough paper
  and pens ready;
- there is enough light, heating, or ventilation for the
  time of day and year;
- there are enough power points, and that they're in
  the right place if you are going to be using an
  overhead projector or laptop;

- any equipment in the room is ready to use and is working properly.

✔ Make further catering arrangements once your numbers are confirmed. If your company has a canteen, book in early for someone to bring tea, coffee and biscuits to the meeting. If you don't have a canteen, ask a colleague or assistant to stay close by at the start of the meeting and to pop out to a nearby coffee shop or café to fetch what is needed. Again, this will free you up to attend to other tasks.

Step four: Keep on track

I Start as you mean to go on

On the day of the meeting, arrive in plenty of time so that you can double-check that everything is ready. Once the attendees have arrived, set the pace and tone of the meeting by following these steps:

✔ Begin on time

✔ Welcome everyone, and briefly explain basic issues such as where the toilets are located (particularly helpful for anyone who hasn't been to your offices before) and what the catering arrangements are

✔ Ask everyone to check that they've turned off their mobile phones so that the flow of discussion isn't interrupted

✔ Reiterate the reason the meeting is being held, what you hope to achieve within the meeting, and the time-scale and finishing time

✔ Frame each item on the agenda by explaining its objectives

2 Keep a tight rein on proceedings

While you need to give everyone an opportunity to contribute to points raised on the agenda, there are steps you can take to make sure that you keep roughly on schedule (and on topic).

✔ Make sure that attendees keep to one agenda point at a time.

✔ Firmly but politely move the discussion on if a subject has become exhausted.

TOP TIP
Sometimes meetings aren't as creative as you may have hoped, and ideas can dry up. If the focus of your meeting is to brainstorm an idea or problem, you may need to kickstart the conversation. To do this, call a 10- or 15-minute break to allow everyone to get some fresh air, make the call they've realised they forgot to make, or just have a change of scenery. Once everyone has returned, set a revised target of ideas for the session

---

('Let's aim to come up with 10 more by lunch'), remind everyone that at this stage, anything goes, and encourage what seem like outlandish ideas. You'll be able to refine these back to something more practical as the discussion progresses, and people will come up with ideas of their own based on others' suggestions.

✔ Don't let one person dominate the conversation. Meetings can often be hijacked by one or two vociferous attendees, so in your role as chair you need to have some strategies to deal with this so that you can both make sure that everyone has a fair say, but also that you keep on schedule.

Strategies for dealing with difficult people

■ **The talkative** – In the case of people who just like the sound of their own voice, you must be assertive enough to interject politely but firmly and remind everyone of the agenda point you're discussing and steer the discussion back to it. Also mention your target finish time and how the meeting is progressing in relation to it.

■ **The passionate** – The same goes for dealing with people who feel very strongly about the issue under discussion and who may feel that others do not share their interest and commitment. Again, make sure that they get the opportunity to voice their point of view, but that they give others the chance to express theirs too. Interject as appropriate and summarise if you sense they are about to repeat something. Remember that a meeting is a discussion with objectives, not an opportunity for attendees to rehearse an extended monologue.

■ **The angry** – If the topic you are discussing is particularly contentious, tempers may flare. If you feel a situation is getting heated and that insults rather than well-considered opinions are being traded, step in to defuse the tension. Suggest a break outside of the meeting room for 15 minutes or so, which will give most people time to calm down and assess what has happened. If voices are being raised, match your voice to the level of other people's, then reduce the volume back down to a normal speaking pitch. This will allow the discussion to get back to a more stable footing.

✔ Make sure that there is only one discussion at a time. Meetings often get sidetracked when some attendees start their own 'private' meeting during the main session. This may range from a few whispered asides, to notes being passed around the table, or a full-blown separate discussion taking place. You'll never finish the main meeting on time if you allow that to happen, so take the initiative to stop these diversions by addressing the people involved directly and asking them if there's something they'd like to raise. For example, you could say: 'I think there may be an issue you're not happy with. Would you like to raise it now before we go any further? We have a lot to get through today.' Be assertive, not aggressive, polite but firm.

✔ Summarise at appropriate intervals and restate agreed action points clearly (the person taking the minutes will be particularly grateful for this).

✔ Wrap up the meeting by thanking everyone for their attendance and contribution. If possible, also let attendees know when the next meeting is to be held (should you need one). This will not only save time on e-mails and phone calls but by giving a sense of continuity and progress, will encourage the attendees not to forget about the topics discussed the moment they leave the room.

Step five: Make sure everyone is clear on any follow-up action required

✔ Ask the person taking the minutes to write them up as soon as possible so that they can be distributed to all the attendees promptly.

Bear in mind that most of the attendees will only glance briefly at the meeting minutes, or refer back to them in order to locate a specific piece of information. This means that they need to be extremely concise and clear. The key things to note are:

- agreed actions;
- the people responsible for them;
- deadlines (if appropriate);
- date of next meeting if you agreed to arrange another.

Common mistakes

✗ You leave preparations to the last minute

You're not saving time by leaving the arrangements for your meeting to the last minute – you're wasting it. The sooner you get started the better as it will save you panicking on the day itself about exactly how many people are coming, if you can cater for them all, where your laptop can be plugged in and other myriad potential nightmares. If you plan in advance, you can make sure everything is in place early and spend the time you'd otherwise be wasting by rushing about aimlessly doing something more productive instead.

✗ You think you can squeeze in taking the minutes

You're not shirking responsibility if you ask someone else to take the meeting's minutes for you. On the contrary, if you are freed up to make sure that the meeting starts and ends on time, is well organised and achieves its objectives, you'll have made everyone's life a lot easier and you'll also end up with a set of minutes (and notes) that mean something.

✗ You lose track of time

Don't be afraid to move things on as appropriate if the meeting seems to be getting bogged down in one particular area. Everyone else will be keen to finish on time and get on with the rest of their day, so, in your role as chair, shape the discussion and sustain the meeting's impetus.

STEPS TO SUCCESS

✔ Only call a meeting if you think one is absolutely necessary

✔ If a meeting does need to be called, give all attendees as much notice as you can

✔ Give yourself plenty of time to book the venue and arrange the necessary catering and equipment

✔ Take time to prepare yourself properly and look over the meeting objectives in advance

✔ On the day of the meeting, arrive on time and begin the meeting on time

✔ Make sure only one discussion is happening at any one time in the room

✔ Give everyone an opportunity to get his or her point across and don't let the conversation be 'hijacked' by one person

✔ Recap action points so that the person taking the minutes is able to note them easily

✔ Keep an eye on the clock and move the meeting on if the attendees are becoming stuck on one particular item

✔ Make sure minutes are circulated promptly after the meeting so that everyone is aware of what is meant to be done when and by whom

Useful links

Meeting Wizard:
www.meetingwizard.com
Vista—Virtual Meetings:
www.vista.uk.com
businessballs.com:
www.businessballs.com/meetings.htm

Keeping on top of e-mail

E-mail has completely changed the way we work today. It offers many benefits and, if used well, can be an excellent tool for improving your own efficiency. Managed badly, though, e-mail can be a waste of valuable time. Statistics indicate that office workers need to wade through an average of more than 30 e-mails a day, while managers or people working on collaborative projects could be dealing with a much higher figure.

This chapter sets out steps to help you manage the time you spend dealing with e-mail so that you can get on with other tasks. It offers help on prioritising those incoming messages and deciding how quickly you need to respond. It tells you how to file an e-mail according to its value or function and encourages you to clear the inbox regularly. Despite your best efforts, unsolicited e-mail or spam can clutter up the most organised inbox and infect your computer system with viruses, so this section gives guidance on protecting yourself. It also suggests alternatives to e-mail that offer the same benefits of speed, convenience and effectiveness.

Step one: Prioritise incoming messages

If you are regularly faced with a large volume of incoming messages, you need to prioritise your inbox. Here is a checklist of tips to help you identify which of the e-mails is really important.

✔ Check the names of the senders. Were you expecting or hoping to hear from them? How quickly do you need to deal with particular individuals?

✔ Check the subject. Is it an urgent issue or just information? Is it about an issue that falls within your sphere of responsibility, or is it something that should just be forwarded to someone else?

✔ Check the priority given by the senders. Do they really mean it's urgent? Remember that some people have a tendency to mark all of their messages 'important', even if they're anything but.

✔ Is it obvious spam? Can it be deleted without reading?

✔ Check the time of the message. Has it been in your inbox a long time?

An initial scan like that can help you identify the e-mails that need your immediate attention. The others can be kept for reading at a more convenient time.

Step two: Reply in stages

Because e-mail is an 'instant' medium, it can be tempting to reply immediately but that might not always be necessary. You can reply in stages, with a brief acknowledgement and a more detailed follow-up. If you do this, give the recipient an indication of when you'll be able to get back to him or her and try to keep to this deadline wherever possible.

✔ If the e-mail simply requires a brief, one line answer then by all means reply immediately. For example, if all you need to say is, 'Yes, I can make the 10.00 meeting', or 'Thanks, that's just the information I needed', do it.

✔ If you are unable to reply there and then or choose not to, let the sender know that you have received the message and will be in touch as soon as possible. This is a useful method of dealing with a query when:

- you need to get further information before replying in full;
- it relates to a relatively complex issue so you need time to consider your response, rather than giving a rushed answer;
- you are angry, upset, frustrated or confused about a message you've received and need a 'cooling-off' period before you make a considered response.

TOP TIP

Taking a staged approach is a useful technique
that allows you to maintain contact while not
interrupting other work that may be more
important. It also gives you a bit of breathing
space if you are feeling under pressure or
worried about the issue under discussion.

Step three: Set specific times for dealing with incoming e-mail

Good time management is essential in all areas of our life
and e-mail is no exception. If you are completely
overwhelmed by the volume of messages in your inbox,
dedicate a certain amount of time each day to sorting
it out.

✔ If you don't work in a traditional office setting you may
have 'dial-up' e-mail where you contact a service
provider to check your inbox. Set a pattern for dialling-in
that fits in well with the type of work you do and the
number of e-mails you expect, and stick to it.

✔ If you have a broadband connection, your computer will
let you know when you receive a new message. Think
about whether to review the new messages immediately
or wait till a pre-determined time. For example, if you
have preferred working patterns or core working hours –

times when you need to be available for contact with overseas clients, for example – you may decide to dedicate a certain portion of the day to dealing with your e-mail.

TOP TIP

If you spend a lot of time in meetings, you may find that you have short spells between meetings (say 10 or 15 minutes) that would otherwise be wasted time. Use these breaks to catch up with your e-mail so that you don't have a flood of them waiting for you at the end of the day.

Step four: Use a filing system to manage your messages

What do you do with incoming messages once you've read them? If the information is important, you may want to keep it for future reference. However, hoarding all your messages in no particular order will not only slow you down when you are looking for information, but is also likely to make your computer system unwieldy and likely to crash.

✔ Check whether your company has a policy for retaining and storing e-mails. Archiving may be essential for legal reasons and if there is a policy in place, you must comply with it. Your company may have a central facility for storing or accessing archived e-mails so investigate with your helpdesk, if you have one. You'll be making their lives easier as well!

If you have a lot of important information you need to hang on to (deals done over e-mail for example, or sign-offs from partners), create your own filing system. For example, you could sort messages into folders arranged by:

■ customer or supplier name
■ project name
■ date of receipt
■ research topic

Use subfolders: for example, for each project it may be useful to subdivide everything into monthly or yearly folders. This will also make it easier to see what should be archived and when.

TOP TIP

To save space in your inbox, you might want to copy important e-mails relating to a specific project or programme into other applications. For example, you could create a Word document called 'project communications', in which all relevant e-mails or messages are held centrally. Everyone will then be able to access the information if you are away for any reason and you will all be able to find what you need quickly.

Step five: Practise good housekeeping

If you don't file your incoming messages as described in Step four, make sure you comb through your inbox regularly. If your inbox is chock-full of every message you've received during the course of a working week, a simple search for an important message could take an awful lot of time.

TOP TIP
Unless you need to keep messages for legal reasons, it's generally good practice to delete them regularly. Regular 'pruning' will help you keep on top of things. To help you do this, some e-mail applications offer an option that asks you if want to empty your deleted items folder every time you exit the application. This useful option will ease you into good e-mail management practice!

✔ Set time limits for keeping messages in your inbox

✔ File or archive any messages that you need to keep

✔ Make sure that you have replied if a response was necessary

✔ Keep any valuable information, such as contact names or phone numbers

✔ Send unwanted messages to the 'deleted messages' section of your e-mail system, but check again before you finally clear that section

Step six: Make arrangements for e-mails when you're away

Opening your inbox after a holiday or a few days away can be an intimidating experience. 'You have 90 new messages' – where do you begin? Step one, 'Prioritise incoming messages', is a good starting point, but a few minutes spent making arrangements before you leave the office will save you a lot of time on your return.

✔ Leave an 'out of office reply' on your system stating when you are back in the office so that your correspondent has a rough idea of how long you'll be away. This responds automatically to incoming e-mails, telling the sender that you are away and will deal with the message on your return. It will not stop the first message from a particular sender, but it may prevent further material or messages from the same person asking why you haven't replied.

✔ If you are expecting a lot of messages or are at a crucial stage in a big project, ask a colleague if you can nominate them to be an alternative point of contact during your absence. If they agree, give his or her e-mail and telephone number in your 'out of office reply'.

✔ Alternatively, ask a colleague to check your inbox regularly for particular types of message and either acknowledge them or deal with the issue, if possible. This will make sure that urgent items receive the right level of attention.

Step seven: Offer alternatives to e-mail

Although e-mail is one of the most popular and convenient ways of communicating quickly, there are practical and effective alternatives:

- Instant Messaging, which allows short messages to be communicated between connected computers on a network. This is ideal for brief communications, such as 'meeting changed to 11.00', or 'send me the latest sales figures'.
- Voicemail, which again allows the caller to leave messages that you can respond to when you're ready.
- Teleconferencing, where a number of people can join in a telephone discussion and make decisions without long e-mail chains.
- Introduction of informal meeting areas which promote real collaboration.

A good deal of e-mail communication comes from external sources, but think about how many e-mails you send each day to your colleagues in the office, or receive from them. Are they all absolutely necessary? If not, why not take the initiative and ask whoever is responsible for company-wide e-mail management to instigate some basic rules that will cut down on internal e-mails? The policies could cover:

- mass copies of e-mail to recipients who don't really need it (for example, sending an e-mail about a project to everyone in the business when only a small group of people need to be kept informed);
- personal e-mail;
- limits on the 'thread' of a discussion which covers every point made by every recipient.

Step eight: Protect against spam

Spam or unwanted e-mail, like the unsolicited direct mail that comes through your letterbox, is a tremendous waste of time and can clog up your e-mail system.

It's a real and growing problem for businesses in the United Kingdom: in December 2003, the Institute for Enterprise and Innovation at the University of Nottingham found that UK office workers spent up to an hour per day deleting spam from their inboxes. That hour could be very well spent tackling other items on your to-do list, so think about the following ways to limit or prevent spam:

✔ Use a filter supplied by your Internet Service Provider. This blocks e-mails that contain certain terms or other attributes that identify the message as potential spam.

✔ If it's practical, set rules for your incoming e-mail. Some rules block all incoming e-mail except messages from addresses you have nominated. This is helpful to a certain degree, but can cause problems for new legitimate contacts or organisations that have changed their addresses.

✔ Unsubscribe to any services or newsletters that you do not wish to receive. The incoming e-mail should provide you with details of how to do this.

✔ Use a separate e-mail address for newsgroups as spammers use these addresses for their mailing lists.

✔ Do not give permission for your e-mail address to be passed on to other parties when you subscribe to or register for a new service. At some stage in the registration or subscription process, you should be asked whether or not you give permission for this to happen, normally in the form of a short statement plus a tick box. Read any such requests very carefully.

✔ As a last resort, change your e-mail address. It might take less time to send a new e-mail address to everyone on your contact list than it does to delete your daily spam load.

TOP TIP

Not only does spam e-mail clog up your inbox,
but it can pass on viruses that may spread
throughout your computer system. You
should immediately delete any e-mail that
you are suspicious of and then empty your
'deleted items' folder. Most companies
will have invested in the most up-to-date
anti-virus software they can afford, but if
you work from home or are self-employed,
it's up to you to make sure your machine is
virus-free. Scan your computer regularly
for viruses and make sure you have the
relevant software and security patches.
The links at the end of the chapter
will help you find out more about this.

Common mistakes

✗ **Reacting immediately to every e-mail**

Like a ringing telephone, it can be hard to ignore a new
incoming message. It takes discipline to wait for a
convenient moment or scan the message and reply later,
but once you have decided on a new approach to
dealing with e-mail, stick to it.

✗ **Not clearing your inbox regularly**

Your list of incoming messages can very quickly grow to
unmanageable proportions. Clear your inbox regularly

or develop a filing system that allows you to respond appropriately and retain useful information.

✗ Not protecting against spam
Spam doesn't just waste your time and fill up your inbox, it can also introduce harmful viruses into your computer or your company network. Make sure you are protected against unwanted e-mail and seek advice from your computer helpdesk team or Internet Service Provider if you have any concerns.

STEPS TO SUCCESS

✔ Prioritise your incoming messages – not every e-mail is urgent or important

✔ Reply when you are ready – an instant medium doesn't require an instant response

✔ Choose a convenient time to deal with non-urgent e-mail

✔ Develop a filing system that allows you to retain and use valuable information

✔ Clear your inbox regularly to prevent your system from becoming unmanageable

✔ Make arrangements to deal with e-mail when you're away from the office so that you don't return to a mountain of messages

✔ Consider alternatives to e-mail such as Instant Messaging, voicemail or face-to-face contact!

✔ Protect yourself against spam by using filters or imposing rules on incoming mail.

Useful links

BBC Webwise:

www.bbc.co.uk/webwise/askbruce

McAfee antivirus software:

www.mcafee.com

Norton AntiVirus software:

www.symantec.com/norton/antivirus

BNET:

www.bnet.com/2410-13068_23-57048.html

Which?

www.which.co.uk/advice/top-email-tips/index.jsp

Maintaining a healthy work–life balance

'Time flies when you're having fun' goes the adage. Time also flies when you are very busy – but rather than having fun, you can soon find yourself stressed in a way that affects not only your mental and emotional wellbeing, but your physical health.

When there isn't enough time in the day, something has to give: but will it be your work or your personal life? Achieving a balance has become one of the burning issues of the day.

Here are some of the main reasons why more and more people are addressing the topic of work–life balance:

- More women joining the workforce means more demands on parents to juggle job and family
- More people living longer means more workers with the care demands of elderly relatives
- More pressure and longer hours at work on account of modern technology (for example, overflowing inboxes, Internet information deluge, and ringing phones) mean people 'burning out' younger

Government figures show that Britain has the longest working hours in Europe, although our workforce is not as productive as those in some countries with shorter hours. So while people are spending more time at work, they are not necessarily achieving more.

The broad argument for greater balance and flexibility at work is that greater satisfaction among employees will lead to fewer stress-related illnesses, less time taken off for sickness, lower staff turnover and higher productivity. People with a good balance between their work and other responsibilities and interests tend to be more motivated and productive: in other words, happy people work better.

Step one: Understand the meaning of work–life balance

Work–life balance is about modifying the way you work in order to accommodate other responsibilities or aspirations. It doesn't only apply to parents of young children or people who need to care for dependents. Quality of life is becoming an issue for everyone.

Thankfully, growing numbers of businesses are becoming aware of the importance of allowing their employees to strike a balance between their work and personal lives. Flexibility in the workplace, moreover, is being driven by business need – working cultures and attitudes are changing in many parts of the world, and many employers see the need to adapt to this if they are to recruit and retain the best people.

Step two: Assess your work-life balance

Planning is essential in gaining a perspective on how your current lifestyle fits in with your ambitions and requirements inside and outside the workplace.

✔ Reflect on your work situation – where you are in terms of your career, how fulfilling you find it, how much of yourself you put into it – and then set yourself some career aims, giving yourself a realistic time scale in which to achieve them.

✔ Consider your personal life. What are the most important elements? Who are the most important people to you? How much are you getting out of it? By asking yourself these profound but crucial questions, you can work out what is lacking in your life and what are unwelcome infringements upon it. Decide what you want to spend more time on, what you want to spend less time on, and then plan how to do it.

It is only once you have established what your aims are and the length of time needed to achieve them, that you can address how changing your work patterns may help you get there.

Step three: Be aware of the options

Find out what your rights are and make sure you're aware of all the choices available to you. Employees now have the right to take periods of paid maternity, paternity and parental leave, as well as the right to take time off (either paid or unpaid, depending on circumstances) to care for dependents. There are, however, several other key areas in which you can address your work–life balance needs and preferences. These are:

I Flexi-time working

People working on flexi-time schedules are able to vary their start and finishing times, providing they work a set number of hours during each week or month.

Flexi-time is not only great for parents trying to manage a household as well as a job, but for anyone who finds working within a strict and continuous routine depressing and demotivating. Everyone's energy levels fluctuate during the day, but not necessarily at the same time, so flexi-time is a good strategy for making sure people always work at their peak. Another great advantage, particularly for city-workers and commuters, is that flexi-time gives you the opportunity to avoid rush-hour – probably one of the most time-wasting and stressful parts of the day.

2 Part-time working

Employees with a part-time arrangement may decide
between working fewer days each week or fewer hours
a day.

This option also works well for people with parental or caring
responsibilities. Other people who benefit greatly from
part-time working are those returning to work after looking
after young children, recovering or suffering from illness
and people who are trying to pursue other interests or
careers.

TOP TIP

**Part-time working should be attainable
without becoming side-lined in the
organisation or losing benefits, such as sick
pay and holiday pay. If you are concerned
about this, you can find out more about your
rights as a part-time employee in the Equal
Pay Act 1970, and get advice from the Equal
Opportunities Commission (www.eoc.org.uk).**

---

3 Job sharing

This involves two people dividing a full-time workload
between them, with each working on a part-time basis. This
is beneficial if you want to maintain something of your career
while being able to spend more time with your children or
pursue interests outside work.

4 Home working or telecommuting

Many jobs now involve computer-based activities that can be done as easily from an Internet-linked PC at home or in a remote (telecommuting) facility. This style of working benefits not only parents and carers, but can help many people without those kinds of domestic responsibilities to work more productively, especially in tasks that require a great deal of concentration, and uninterrupted peace and quiet away from colleagues, phones, day-to-day admin and work e-mails. It is unusual for someone to work from home or remotely full-time, but some employers do find it a cost advantage through the reduced need for fixed office space.

5 Term-time working

This option allows employees to take time off work during school holidays in order to look after their children. This time off is usually taken as unpaid leave, although the salary can be paid evenly across the year. The sorts of employers most likely to operate this scheme are those in industries that experience seasonal peaks and troughs.

6 Other options

The variety of opportunities being adopted by organisations to help you achieve the right balance does not stop there. The Department for Business Innovation and Skills (BIS) website has a fairly comprehensive list (see Useful links at the end of the chapter). In addition to the options outlined above, it includes:

- Staggered hours: staff work to different start, finish and break times
- Compressed working hours: staff work their total weekly number of hours over fewer days
- Annualised hours: staff have more flexibility about taking time off as working hours are calculated over the year rather than by the week
- Shift swapping: staff negotiate their working times and shifts between themselves
- Self-rostering: staff state their preferred working times, and then shifts are organised to accommodate as many of those preferences as possible
- Career breaks: as well as paternity, maternity and parental leave, staff may also be allowed unpaid career breaks and sabbaticals
- Time off in lieu (TOIL): staff are given time off when they have put in extra hours at work
- Flexible and cafeteria benefits: staff are offered a choice of benefits so that they can pick those best suited to them

Step four: Make an application for flexible working hours

I Find out how the processes work

✔ First of all, make sure that you qualify for flexible working arrangements. Most people apply for flexible working because of their family situation. As of April 2003 and

under the terms of the Employment Act 2002, parents
of children under the age of six, or of less abled-bodied
children under the age of 18, may request flexible working
hours, but they need to have completed six months'
continuous service at the company or organisation in
question before making that request. Some
organisations may also consider flexible working if you
need to care for a dependent adult, such as your
spouse, partner or parent.

✔ Check the employees' handbook or with your human
resources department (if you have one) to see what the
preferred method of application is. BIS has some basic
forms that may be customised, so your company may
be using these already. If not, most companies would
expect a request for a change in working hours to be
made in writing. This should be followed up within
28 days by a meeting between you and your manager.
Bear in mind that only one application can be made in
any 12-month period.

✔ Do some informal research. Once you've checked out
your company's policy, speak to friends or colleagues
who have applied for flexible working hours or who
are already working under a new arrangement. How did
the successful applicants approach their request? Are
they finding it easier or harder than they'd anticipated to
work in a new way? Bear in mind that if your working
arrangements are changed, these changes are
permanent unless otherwise agreed between you and
your employer.

2 Make a persuasive case

✔ Prepare your case and try to anticipate the questions your manager may ask you when you meet to talk about your application. Requests can be turned down because managers fear that flexible working arrangements may affect the business, so be prepared to give well-thought-out, positive responses to questions such as:

- Will you still be an effective team member?
- How would a change in your working hours affect your colleagues?
- What will be the overall effect on the work you do?
- How could a change in your working hours affect the business positively?

TOP TIP
Be realistic and also be ready to compromise. A popular way of approaching negotiations of any type is to draw up a wish-list for your successful outcome that contains an ideal solution, a realistic one and an absolute minimum. If you show that you are prepared to be flexible, your manager may be willing to meet you half way.

✔ Think about when you would want any new arrangement to start and give your company as much notice as you can. This will convey the fact that you are still committed to the company and are thinking about how the potential changes to your working life will fit in overall.

✔ Stress that the quality of your work and your motivation will not change, even if your working hours do. In fact, you'll be more productive as you'll suffer from less stress and will need to take fewer days off sick to look after your children or dependents when they are ill. You could also explain that as part of a reciprocal arrangement whereby all parties benefit, you'd be willing to work extra or longer in times of heavy demand. Finally, but no less importantly, explain how much knowledge and expertise you have built up while you have been working there and how much the company benefits from it.

TOP TIP

Many companies or organisations will allow you to bring a union representative with you to a meeting to discuss your application. If you do invite one along, make sure he or she has read a copy of your application and any related documents from your place of work and is up to speed.

---

3 Follow up

According to the BIS guidelines, you should be informed about the outcome of your application within 14 days of your meeting.

✔ If all goes well and an agreement is reached, your new working arrangement and an agreed start date should be set down in writing and copies given to all relevant parties (you, your manager and the HR department or representative if you have one).

✔ If your request is not granted, you may appeal within 14 days of receiving the decision. See the BIS website (www.bis.gov.uk) for further advice on this issue.

Step five: Set up a flexible working system in your organisation

If you are an employer or manager, be prepared for some extra administrative costs involved in, for example, setting up IT equipment at home for employees. It's important to remember though, that the benefits of retaining skilled and experienced staff should outweigh these costs, not least in reducing the expense of recruiting and training replacements for dissatisfied employees who have chosen to leave.

1 Think about the needs of the business

Start by clarifying the most important needs of your business. Flexible working will only be sustainable if it does not hinder your business's ability to perform efficiently and profitably.

✔ Speak to your staff to find out how many of them are interested in exploring flexible working arrangements.

✔ Engage staff in thinking about how flexible arrangements would affect the business and customers. Discuss what sort of re-organisation might be involved in new working arrangements.

✔ Ensure that your staff understand what the business needs from them, so that they do not make unrealistic requests about working flexibly.

TOP TIP
If you're an employer worried that your business won't be able to cope if all the employees decide they want to work flexible hours, you can relax. The evidence so far suggests that only a small proportion of people adopt flexible working arrangements. By consulting with your employees before new arrangements are introduced, you can avoid resentment developing and ensure that flexibility works to everyone's advantage.

---

2 Develop and implement a policy
✔ Formulate a policy on how your business views flexible working. Discuss these ideas with staff as you formulate them, so that they see the policy developing and feel they have been consulted in the process.

✔ Write down a procedure for how you will deal with requests for flexible arrangements, and how staff performance will be monitored. Make sure everyone is aware of these procedures.

✔ Implement your plans over a trial period.

✔ Together with staff, review how well the process works, and assess the impact of flexible working on the business.

✔ Make necessary changes to your policy or practices; monitor and review these regularly.

TOP TIP
As an employer, the key to making flexible arrangements work is setting and monitoring the workload and tasks for employees working from home. If proper trust is established and workloads or tasks are agreed and monitored, there should be no need for direct supervision.

Common mistakes

As an employee:
✘ **You don't prepare well enough**
As with all types of negotiation, you need to make sure that you've done your groundwork when you make an

application for flexible working hours. First, be aware of your rights by researching the issue: you might want to visit the BIS website which sets out the rights and responsibilities of both employers and employees. Second, check your company's stance on the issue, and make sure you follow the procedures properly when submitting a written application. When you meet your manager to discuss the application, stress that your commitment to your role and the company will not change, and think through questions he or she might ask you about the effects of flexible working on your workload and that of your colleagues.

✗ You aren't flexible

Bear in mind that the legislation relating to flexible working hours gives you the right to *request* them: it doesn't mean that your company will necessarily agree to your application, although they have a responsibility to consider it reasonably. If you are flexible when you meet with your manager and open to compromise if your ideal scenario is not possible, then it's more likely that you'll end up with a result that suits everyone.

✗ You don't think through all the financial implications

Don't forget that when you reduce your hours, it's not just your salary that may be affected. Pension contributions and other benefits may change too. Be sure that when you take the decision to apply for flexible working hours, you'll be able to cope financially if your application is granted.

As an employer:

✗ You try to implement change too quickly

Moving towards a work–life balance, and bringing about a cultural change, doesn't happen overnight. Strive initially to create an environment of openness and mutual respect, where individuals gradually feel a sense of support and trust. From there you can move towards a balance between the demands of your business and the personal needs of your employees.

✗ You begrudge employees who want a flexible working arrangement

Employees who make choices that support a work–life balance shouldn't feel a sense of disapproval, nor that they can no longer expect to progress within your organisation. Be inclusive and avoid alienating people with particular personal needs.

✗ You lose touch with out-of-office staff

Staff who aren't in the office regularly may start feeling isolated. Try to avoid this by planning regular feedback meetings in the office, and organising social events to bring staff together.

STEPS TO SUCCESS

✔ When assessing your work–life balance, decide upon your career aims and personal ambitions and how long you think you need in order to achieve them.

✓ Find out about all the various flexible working options available. Consider which one would suit the needs of your desired lifestyle best.

✓ An application for flexible working needs to be well researched. You should prepare your case thoroughly so that the employer feels reassured that you have the business's best interests at heart as well as your own.

✓ Employers should take a planned approach to implementing flexible working arrangements, involving consultations with staff to decide on the best policy.

✓ Flexible working policy should be implemented over a trial period, and followed up with a review of how it is working and adjustments to ensure that the business continues to function efficiently.

Useful links

Department for Business Innovation & Skills:
www.bis.gov.uk
Employers for Work–Life Balance:
www.employersforwork-lifebalance.org.uk
Flexibility.co.uk:
www.flexibility.co.uk/issues/WLB/index.htm
The Work Foundation:
**www.theworkfoundation.com/research/health/
worklifebalance.aspx**

Developing decision-making skills

Some people are naturally more decisive than others. For them, it's relatively easy to respond to a situation, weigh up the pros and cons of various ways of tackling the issue, make the decision and move on. For the indecisive, though, the process can be nightmarish, stressful and eat up an awful lot of valuable time. The trick here is to find a decision-making style that means you spend enough time on a decision to make sure it's a good, well-considered one, but that you cut out the procrastination. Avoid the temptation to make knee-jerk judgments: you may think you are creating a good impression by looking decisive, but it's the quality of the decision that counts in the end.

This chapter sets out to help you if you find decision-making a challenge. While you may not always be able to predict or control the everyday circumstances that you face, and, clearly, some decisions are a lot easier to make than others, there are skills you can learn that will improve how you respond. As you practise these skills and habits, they will gradually become second nature. The result will be less stress, more decisiveness, less time wasted and more focus in your working life.

To make the best decision possible, be clear about your goals, the problem in question, the options open to you, the possible consequences, the timescale and the outcome of previous decisions on the matter. The process combines your intuition (to initiate your response and come up with innovative options) and your analytical ability (with which you scrutinise and quantify your options).

Step one: Understand what you want your decision to achieve

When you are faced with a difficult issue, try to look past your immediate objective and take in your longer-term goals as well. For example, let's say you work in sales and have dealings with a wide variety of customers. If one of your customers wants you to drop your price to an uneconomical level, think about how important the sale is in the long run. If that customer does not feature in your business priorities, then you might only damage your reputation among competitors and other customers by dropping your price too low. On the other hand, if the customer is in a sector that you want to break in to, then a low-margin sale may give you an important foot in the door for future business.

✔ Once you have defined the objectives of your decision, then you are in a position to determine its level of significance. This is important for deciding the amount of time and resources you should spend in making the right decision.

Different decision levels

1 Strategic

Decisions about strategy are concerned with long-term goals, philosophies and the overall scheme of masterminding the future direction of the business. They therefore tend to be more theoretical than practical, more unpredictable in outcome and more risky. This gives them great importance.

2 Tactical

Tactical decisions are concerned with short- to medium-term objectives, and usually involve the implementation of strategic decisions and planning. The long-term risks are fewer and the significance, therefore, more moderate. However, as tactical decisions turn strategic decisions into reality they are more likely to involve the overseeing and handling of budgets, people, schedules and resources, which represents a considerable responsibility.

3 Operational

Operational decisions are concerned with day-to-day systems and procedures and so tend to be more structured – to the extent that they can be routine or pre-programmed. As the third level down in the decision food chain they are used to support tactical decisions. The outcomes of operational decisions therefore tend to be immediate- to short-term, and involve few risks. Nevertheless, a series of decision errors can have a knock-on effect, with repercussions far beyond the purely operational sphere.

Step two: Find the information you need

✓ Give yourself as much time as you can to research the issue surrounding the decision you need to make. Try to resist as far as possible the temptation to promise a quick decision.

✓ Identify which sources of information you will need and make sure that they can be accessed quickly and easily. Get advice from experts or colleagues, and be honest about those areas where you do not have the answers.

✓ Wherever possible, cut out assumptions: check your facts. This might look like an extra hoop to jump through, but it is a valuable one. If you base a decision around a factor or number of factors that actually turn out to be unreliable, you'll have wasted hours of work anyway.

TOP TIP
Ask for help from your colleagues or manager
if time is very short or you've reached an
impasse – a brainstorming session is often a
good idea and often people who are new to
an issue may see a solution that you've
overlooked because you're so close to it.

Six thinking hats

This powerful technique, developed by lateral thinking
pioneer, Edward de Bono, will help you to look at
decisions from many perspectives.

✓ Allocate each individual – alone or in a group – a
series of imaginary hats, which represent different
outlooks, according to colour. This forces people to
move into different modes of thinking.

- White hats focus on the data, look for gaps,
extrapolate from history and examine future
trends.
- Red hats use intuition and emotion to look at
problems.
- Black hats look at the negative, and find reasons
why something may not work. If an idea can
get through this process, it's more likely to
succeed.

- Yellow hats think positively. This hat's optimistic view helps you to see the benefits of a decision, providing a boost to the thinking process.
- Green hats develop creative, freewheeling solutions. There is no room for criticism in this mode; it's strictly positive.
- Blue hats orchestrate the meeting – you're in control in this hat. Feel free to propose a new hat to keep ideas flowing.

Step three: Outline the alternatives and their consequences

✔ Get a few options down in writing, then explore the positive and negative consequences of each; give special attention to the unintended consequences that might arise, especially if you are considering a course of action that you have not tried before. You may find it useful to list these in columns alongside the options.

✔ Make sure you analyse all the main alternatives and their consequences in this way. Your analysis at this stage may prove valuable further down the line when you might have to justify why you chose one course of action over another.

TOP TIP

Force field analysis is useful for examining pros and cons. By looking at the forces that will support or challenge a decision (such as finances or market conditions), you can strengthen the pros and diminish the cons. Draw three columns, and place the situation or issue in the middle. The pros push on one side, and the cons push on the other. Allocate scores to each force to convey its potency. This allows you to measure the overall advantages and disadvantages of any given action. SWOT analysis is another handy grid technique that works by identifying the Strengths and Weaknesses of a decision, and examining the existing Opportunities and Threats. You can find more information on these techniques online (see Useful links at the end of this chapter).

Step four: Judge each alternative by your goals

✔ Go back to what you wanted your decision to achieve; that is, remind yourself of what your priorities are in this situation. This forces you to always consider your longer-term goals when making your shorter-term decisions, and ensures that they are 'pointing in the same direction'.

✔ Measure the merits and problems in each alternative – this may be a case of estimating financial costs and benefits, or it may involve less tangible factors like goodwill or publicity. This involves a forward-thinking process of predicting what will happen as a result of your decision. Make a note of these expectations, as they will be important when you review your decision later on and judge with hindsight whether it was a good one.

✔ Compare the alternatives to each other, and decide which one comes out best in the light of the information available.

TOP TIP

Decision trees are a great way to help you examine alternative solutions and their impact, especially when decisions are required in situations where there is a great deal of information to sift through. Start your decision tree on one side of a piece of paper, with a symbol representing the decision to be made. Different lines representing various solutions open out like a fan from this nexus. Additional decisions or uncertainties that need to be resolved are indicated on these lines and, in turn, form the new decision point, from which yet more options fan out.

Step five: Take the decision, and implement it

✔ Make sure that everyone involved is informed about the decision you have taken; the value of a good decision is often undermined if your staff or colleagues hear about it through inappropriate channels. You will normally need to inform the more senior people first, but speed is often of the essence when letting people know; plan your timing carefully and control the process firmly.

✔ Explain the reasons why the decision was made, especially when the decision is contentious. Outline what benefits you expect as a result, as well as any other implications that the business needs to anticipate.

✔ Get the right people on to the job of implementing the decision, so that it gets the best possible chance of success.

Step six: Review the consequences of your decision

✔ Estimate how long it will take before the decision will have an effect, and plan an assessment at that time to review how well it went. Make sure that some measurement is being made that you can use later to help in your assessment. If it's a decision to send out a promotional mailing, for instance, then ensure that someone is collecting information on the impact of that mailing on daily orders.

The review should be a learning exercise – not just for you but for everyone concerned with making the decision and implementing it. Try and get as many of these people as possible involved in the review process. This will help them when a similar decision needs to be taken next time; it will also advance their own decision-making skills and enhance their value to the business.

Common mistakes

✗ You put off making a difficult decision
Procrastination will seldom lead to a decision becoming easier to make. Give the decision some thought as early as you can, and give yourself a deadline for making it, based on how long you think you need to gather the necessary information and input, and how important a decision it is.

✗ You make snap decisions under pressure
Making any decision without enough thought is risky; if you are in a pressurised office situation and time is short, there is the added danger of not being able to see the whole picture. In a quick decision, you may neglect to think through important consequences of your actions.

✗ You don't consult those who will be affected

Nothing is quite as demotivating for staff as feeling
that their input is not valued or their feelings are not
respected. Before you begin to address a decision,
think carefully about each of the people who are – or
could later be – affected by the outcome of your
decision. Make sure that you include them, not
necessarily all of them at every step, but leave them in
no doubt that their input is appreciated.

**✗ You let your bad decisions overshadow your
good ones**

No one can get it right 100% of the time, and there are
bound to be occasions when your decisions do not
have the effect you'd hoped for or intended. Try not to
be too downcast by this, and see bad decisions as
part of the learning process, not as indications of failure.
If you learn from a bad decision, that in itself is a good
outcome. Don't be too hard on yourself.

STEPS TO SUCCESS

✔ Clarify why you want to take the decision, and what
benefits you expect to flow from it.

✔ Get others involved in making the decision if they will be
affected by it, to contribute information and alternatives.

✔ Consider using a range of established techniques like
six thinking hats, force field analysis, decision trees and

SWOT analysis, to help you cover all the options and assess their likely effectiveness.

✔ Plan what needs to be done in implementing the decision fully, so that everyone involved feels part of it.

✔ Make time to review the decision and make changes if the outcome is not what you had hoped.

Useful links

businessballs.com:
www.businessballs.com/problemsolving.htm
Mind Tools:
www.mindtools.com
Time Management Guide:
www.time-management-guide.com/decision-making-skills.html
Virtual Salt:
www.virtualsalt.com/crebook6.htm

Where to find more help

30 Minutes to Manage Information Overload
John Caunt
London: Kogan Page, 1999
64pp ISBN: 0749429801
This is a brief but useful source of help for anyone feeling
overwhelmed by the amount of information he or she needs to
manage at work. Covering both traditional and online information,
this book offers practical hints on reviewing the way you work
currently and processing and storing information more efficiently.

Downshifting: How to Work Less and Enjoy Life More
John D. Drake
San Francisco: Berrett-Koehler, 2001
136pp ISBN: 1576751163
This is a thought-provoking book aimed at anyone unhappy with
their current work–life balance. It offers advice to those thinking of
changing their life to a less work-centred one but also gives time
management help to readers coping with long working days.

Get Everything Done and Still Have Time to Play
Mark Forster
London: Hodder & Stoughton, 2000
208pp ISBN: 0340746203
Based on the author's view that time can't be managed, but that
you can change the way you focus on tasks so that you make the
best use of time available, this book offers advice on how to
prioritise, plan, allocate time-slots to different activities and
overcome your natural resistance to some of the demands on your
day-to-day life.

Getting Things Done: The Art of Stress-free Productivity
David Allen
London: Penguin Books, 2003
267pp ISBN: 978–0142000281
This book offers a system for downloading all those floating tasks

into a framework of files and action lists. With his ingenious Two minute Rule – if there's anything you absolutely must do that you can do right now in two minutes or less, then do it now, thus freeing up your time and mind tenfold over the long term – the author underlines the common sense behind being organised that most of us overlook, much to our detriment.

The One-Minute Manager
Kenneth H. Blanchard and Spencer Johnson Rev ed.
London: HarperCollins Entertainment 2000
112pp ISBN: 0007107927
Kenneth Blanchard has written many books based on the perennially popular idea of the one-minute manager. This accessible book aims to help anyone fix goals and objectives so that they can organise their lives better, work more effectively and live with others more harmoniously.

Manage meetings positively: How to take charge and come up with results
London: A & C Black, 2006
96pp ISBN: 0713675233
Are you meeting-phobic? Spending hours of your precious time locked up in pointless meetings can be a nightmare. If your job means that you have to chair meetings, you'll need to know how to contend with difficult situations too. Whatever your meeting-related worries, this book will help you get to grips with them. It covers a range of key issues, from the basics, to coping with fraught discussions, meeting with people from other business cultures and getting the best from virtual meetings.

Time Management from the Inside Out
Julie Morgenstern
London: Hodder & Stoughton, 2001
239pp ISBN: 0340771380
This is a thorough, accessible guide to creating a time management system that works for you and your personal situation. The author sets out to give sound advice that can be customised across a range of lifestyles.